MAMMALS

by
Charlie Ogden

KidHaven PUBLISHING

Published in 2017 by
KidHaven Publishing, an Imprint of Greenhaven Publishing, LLC
353 3rd Avenue
Suite 255
New York, NY 10010

© 2017 Booklife Publishing
This edition is published by arrangement with Booklife Publishing

Designer: Danielle Jones
Editor: Grace Jones

Cataloging-in-Publication Data
Names: Ogden, Charlie.
Title: Mammals / Charlie Ogden.
Description: New York : KidHaven Publishing, 2017. | Series: Animal classification | Includes index.
Identifiers: ISBN 9781534520172 (pbk.) | ISBN 9781534520196 (library bound) | ISBN 9781534520189 (6 pack) | ISBN 9781534520202 (ebook)
Subjects: LCSH: Mammals–Juvenile literature.
Classification: LCC QL706.2 O37 2017 | DDC 599–dc23

Printed in the United States of America

CPSIA compliance information: Batch #CW17KL: For further information contact Greenhaven Publishing LLC, New York, New York at 1-844-317-7404.

Please visit our website, www.greenhavenpublishing.com. For a free color catalog of all our high-quality books, call toll free 1-844-317-7404 or fax 1-844-317-7405.

Photo Credits
Abbreviations: l–left, r–right, b–bottom, t–top, c–center, m–middle.

Front Cover – davemhuntphotography. Back Cover – suradach. 2 – Tom Grundy. 4l – Marques. 4b – Philip Evans. 5 – pandapaw. 6m – outdoorsman. 6bl – Vladimir Melnik. 7l – tsuneomp. 7r – Thomas Ash. 8 – Jean-Edouard Rozey. 9t – cynoclub. 9m – Asparuh. 9b – Kseniia Mitus. 10 – nevodka. 10tl – Neirfy. 10m – belizar. 10b – bimserd. 11t – Eric Isselee. 11b – Johannes Kornelius. 11bl – Anan Kaewkhammul. 12tl – Tilo G. 12b – Africa Studio. 12br – Eric Isselee. 13t – Sebastian Kaulitzki. 13b – jan zalsky. 14tl – Eric Isselee. 14tm – Coffeemill. 14tr – Max K. 14bl – Michal Ninger. 14bm – Sharon Morris. 14br – Eric Pavel Hlystov. 15t – Mogens Trolle. 15b - antpkr. 15bl – Studio DMM Photography, Designs & Art. 15br – Drakuliren. 16rt – Joel Shawn. 16b – Lorna Roberts. 17t – BOONCHUAY PROMJIAM Vladimirovich. 17b – Ivan Kuzmin. 18t – Lenar Musin. 18b – Anan Kaewkhammul. 19t – Ondrej Prosicky. 19b – gillmar. 19br – @erics. 19bl – gillmar. 20 – mariait. 21t – By Stefan Kraft [GFDL (http://www.gnu.org/copyleft/fdl.html) or CC-BY-SA-3.0 (http://creativecommons.org/licenses/by-sa/3.0/)], via Wikimedia Commons. 21b – Eric Isselee. 22t – kbremote. 22b – Dr_Flash. 23t – Artush. 23b – Stuart G Porter. 24b – Andreas Argirakis. 24bl – volkova natalia. 25t – Chuck Rausin. 25b – By Solenodon joe (Own work) [CC BY 3.0 (http://creativecommons.org/licenses/by/3.0)], via Wikimedia Commons. 26t – Vladimir Wrangel. 26b – Erwin Niemand. 27t – By Olga Shpak (http://ria.ru/earth/20140219/995484804.html) [CC BY-SA 3.0 (http://creativecommons.org/licenses/by-sa/3.0)], via Wikimedia Commons. 27b – Clinton Hastings. 28bl – bikeriderlondon. 28br – angelo lano. 29 – Kodda. Images are courtesy of Shutterstock.com, unless stated otherwise. With thanks to Getty Images, Thinkstock Photo, and iStockphoto.

CONTENTS

Words that are underlined are explained in the glossary on page 31.

THE ANIMAL KINGDOM

The animal kingdom includes more than 8 million known living species. They come in many different shapes and sizes, they each do weird and wonderful things, and they live all over Earth.

From the freezing Arctic waters to the hottest desert in the world, animals have adapted to the often extreme and diverse conditions on Earth.

Even though each and every species is <u>unique</u>, they all still share certain characteristics with each other. These shared characteristics are used to classify animals. There are six main groups used to classify animals. They are mammals, reptiles, birds, insects, amphibians, and fish.

10,000 new species of animals are discovered **every year.**

This elephant is a mammal.

MAMMALS

WHAT IS A MAMMAL?

A mammal is a type of animal that breathes air using lungs, has a backbone, and generally grows fur on its body.

Most mammals give birth to live babies and produce milk to feed their babies. Mammals are warm-blooded animals, which means they maintain a stable body temperature, even if they live in a very hot or very cold <u>habitat</u>.

Polar bears maintain a stable body temperature even when the temperature outside is below freezing because they are warm-blooded animals.

There are around 5,000 known species of mammals alive today. They come in many different shapes and sizes, and they each have their own individual features that help them survive in their habitats. Humans, lions, elephants, and dolphins are all types of mammals.

blue whale

Etruscan shrew

The largest mammal on Earth is the blue whale, which is about 100 feet (30 m) long. The Etruscan shrew is the smallest mammal on Earth, measuring in at just 1.6 inches (4 cm) long.

MAMMAL CHECKLIST

- 🐾 gives birth to live babies
- 🐾 produces milk to feed babies
- 🐾 has fur on its body (most mammals)
- 🐾 is warm-blooded
- 🐾 breathes air using lungs
- 🐾 is a <u>vertebrate</u>

BODY PARTS

Mammals come in a lot of different shapes and sizes, which can make it difficult to determine whether an animal is a mammal or not! However, there are a few <u>traits</u> that all mammals share with one another.

This doesn't mean that every mammal has to have every one of these traits—science can't always be perfect! Instead, it means if an animal has most or all of these traits, then it is probably a mammal.

Many mammals use their fur to keep their body temperature stable in cold <u>climates</u>.

teeth

mammary
glands

One example of a mammal
that has all of these common
traits is a dog. Dogs have
four <u>limbs</u> they use to get
around. Female dogs also
have mammary glands that
produce milk, which they feed
their babies with.

fur

limbs

Most mammals can only lose their
teeth once, often when they are still
young. After this, their teeth must
last for the rest of their lives.

ODD ONES OUT

Some animals don't have all of these common traits but are still classified as mammals.

Dolphins are mammals even though they don't have four limbs or fur! One reason they are still mammals is because they can't breathe underwater like fish. Instead, they need to come to the surface to breathe air through their <u>blowholes</u>.

blowhole

Some **dolphins** can hold their breath for up to 30 minutes!

naked mole rat

Naked mole rats are mammals even though they don't have fur. This is because they're warm-blooded and give birth to live babies.

koala

Some traits are only found in a few mammals and not in any other <u>class</u> of animal. One of these traits is a pouch on the stomach where females keep their babies. Mammals that have this pouch are called marsupials, and they're generally found in Australia. A marsupial baby is very weak when it's born, so its mother must keep it in the pouch and feed it milk until it gets stronger. Kangaroos and koalas are both marsupials.

Kangaroos move by jumping forward with both feet at once. This means kangaroos can't walk backward!

GETTING AROUND

Mammals move in different ways depending on their habitat. Mammals that only live in trees, such as monkeys, koalas, and sloths, are known as arboreal mammals. These mammals use their bodies in amazing ways to move through the trees.

sloth

A group of **monkeys** is called a **troop.**

Monkeys have long limbs, sharp claws, and strong hands, which make it easier for them to grip and swing between branches. They also have a prehensile tail, which is a tail that can grip things. Monkeys use their prehensile tail for balance and as an extra way to hold on to trees.

BREATHING

All mammals, including humans, breathe using <u>organs</u> called lungs. The lungs pull in and push out air with the help of the diaphragm, which is a muscle that sits just under the rib cage. <u>Oxygen</u> enters the body through the mouth and nose, flows through the larynx, fills the lungs, and passes into the <u>bloodstream</u>.

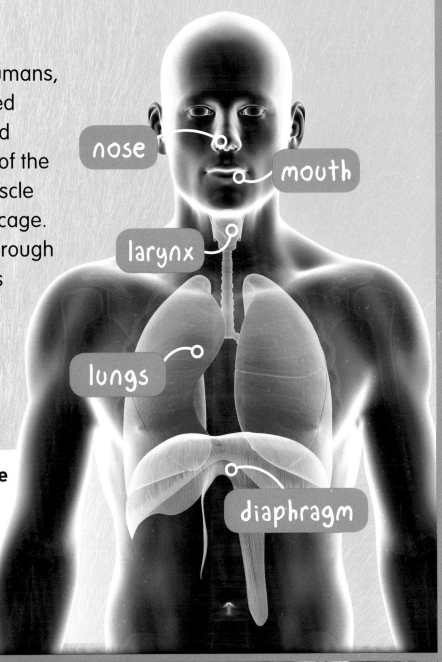

nose

mouth

larynx

lungs

diaphragm

Hiccups are caused by the diaphragm moving when it's not supposed to. This is why you quickly breathe in when you hiccup.

PREDATORS AND PREY

All animals can be sorted into groups depending on what they eat. The three groups are carnivores, herbivores, and omnivores.

herbivores
plant eaters

carnivores
meat eaters

omnivores
plant and meat eaters

canine teeth

Carnivores often have long canine teeth that they use to tear off pieces of meat. The teeth furthest back in the mouth, called molars, will often be flat and <u>blunt</u> in herbivores. These teeth are better for crushing and grinding plants. Omnivores often have both of these types of teeth, and they will use their teeth differently depending on what they're eating.

Animals that hunt other animals are called predators, whereas animals that are hunted by other animals are called prey.

It's possible for a mammal to be neither a predator nor prey. Moose are herbivores, which means they don't hunt other creatures, and they're generally too big to be the prey of any other animal. It's also possible for a mammal to be both a predator and prey, such as the weasel. Weasels eat smaller mammals, such as mice, rats, and rabbits, but are often hunted by larger mammals, such as foxes.

LAND, SEA, AND SKY

Mammals can be found in almost every habitat on land—from jungles and forests to deserts and mountains. However, only a few mammals are able to live in water or in the sky.

Sea otters spend most of their lives floating on their back in the ocean, and they use their thick fur to stay warm.

Sea otters often use rocks to break open the shellfish they find. Sea otters and other mammals that live in water are known as aquatic mammals.

Otters are one of the only animals that use tools! Can you think of any others?

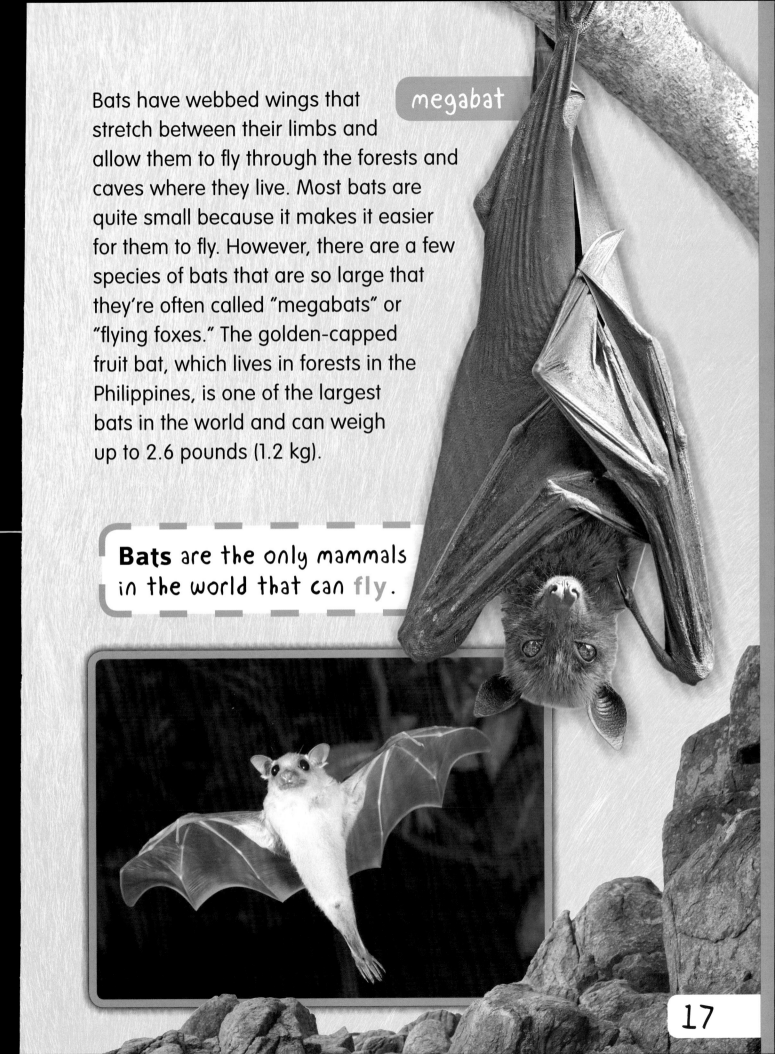

Bats have webbed wings that stretch between their limbs and allow them to fly through the forests and caves where they live. Most bats are quite small because it makes it easier for them to fly. However, there are a few species of bats that are so large that they're often called "megabats" or "flying foxes." The golden-capped fruit bat, which lives in forests in the Philippines, is one of the largest bats in the world and can weigh up to 2.6 pounds (1.2 kg).

megabat

Bats are the only mammals in the world that can **fly**.

ADAPTATION

Some mammals have adapted to their extreme habitats in amazing ways

DESERTS

Living in the desert can be dangerous because the high temperatures and dry climate make it difficult to find water. It's easy to become dehydrated in desert climates. Dehydration occurs when the body doesn't have enough water. If an animal becomes dehydrated, they can die in a matter of hours.

Some desert mammals, such as the porcupine, have adapted by becoming <u>nocturnal</u>, which means they look for food and water at night when it's cooler.

The long, thick, and sharp hairs on a porcupine are called quills, and each porcupine has around 30,000 of them.

18

THE ARCTIC

Mammals that live in the Arctic have different problems.

Here there is very little food and temperatures often fall below -40° Fahrenheit (-40° Celsius). To survive the extreme cold in the Arctic, polar bears have developed smaller ears than other bears, which reduces how much heat they lose.

The polar bear's heavy coat of fur and thick layer of fat also help keep it warm. When it becomes difficult to find food, a polar bear uses its layer of fat as an emergency store of energy.

Polar bears are the **largest land predators** in the world.

19

LIFE CYCLES

The life cycle of an animal is the series of changes that it goes through from the start to the end of its life.

Possibly the most important part of every life cycle is reproduction, which involves the <u>fertilization</u> process and how babies develop. For nearly all mammals, the fertilization process occurs inside the female's body, and then the female gives birth to live babies instead of laying eggs. The mother feeds the baby or babies the milk it produces in its mammary glands.

Elephant mothers feed their babies for up to four years.

The platypus has a bill like a duck, a tail like a beaver, and feet like an otter!

The two mammals that lay eggs instead of giving birth to live babies are the platypus and the echidna. The way these mammals reproduce is similar to reptiles, which also lay eggs. However, the platypus and the echidna are still mammals, as they have mammary glands and they feed milk to their babies once they hatch from their eggs. Both of these animals are only found in the wild in Australia and on some nearby islands.

The echidna has spines like a porcupine and a nose like an anteater!

LIFE CYCLE OF A ZEBRA

egg

Zebra mothers carry their babies in their body for 13 months, which is 4 months longer than human mothers. This gives the baby more time to grow and means that zebras are able to walk around within an hour of being born.

Zebras go back to living in herds when they're ready to have their own babies. Male zebras, called stallions, return to the herd at 3½ years old. Female zebras, called mares, sometimes don't return to their herds until they're 6 years old. Mares can give birth up to six times during their lives.

adulthood

foal

Baby zebras, known as foals, stay close to their mother for the first few weeks after they're born. A foal will drink its mother's milk for the first three months of its life.

colt

After nearly two years, young zebras will leave their <u>herd</u> to live alone or with other young zebras called colts. It's during this time that zebras learn how to find food and water for themselves.

EXTREME MAMMALS

Some mammals have developed extreme habits or skills that help them survive.

BROWN BEAR

Every autumn, brown bears start to eat as much food as they can find. This gives the bear a thick layer of fat that it can survive on for the entire winter. In October or November, the brown bear crawls into a hole or a cave and sleeps for the next four to seven months.

While a brown bear sleeps during the winter, its heartbeat becomes very slow, and it can lose up to 40 percent of its body weight.

Size:
up to 9.8 feet
(3 m) long

Home:
forests and
mountains in
North America,
northern Europe,
and northern Asia

Diet:
fruit, roots,
bulbs, and fish

SOLENODON

Animals that are venomous protect themselves from other creatures by injecting them with a harmful substance through a bite or a sting. Most venomous animals, such as snakes, are reptiles, but some mammals are venomous, too! Solenodons have special teeth that inject venom into their prey or creatures that are attacking them—just like snakes! Solenodon venom isn't strong enough to kill a person, but it would still be extremely painful.

venomous fangs

Size:
11.8 inches
(30 cm) long

Home:
Hispaniola
and Cuba

Diet:
insects and
worms

Solenodons are hard to find because they live underground and are nocturnal. They weren't seen for so long that some people believed there were none left.

HONEY BADGER

Honey badgers are one of the fiercest animals in the world.

Honey badgers prey on venomous snakes and scorpions, and they're often bitten or stung while hunting. This would kill most other animals, but honey badgers are able to survive the venom. Honey badgers are not scared of anything and have been known to attack much larger animals when they feel threatened—even lions! The honey badger's extremely thick and rubbery skin helps it avoid serious injury when it attacks.

Size: 2.5 feet (0.75 m) long
Home: Africa, Iran, and India
Diet: honey, eggs, turtles, rodents, and snakes

The skin of a honey badger is so strong that arrows and spears can't hurt it.

WHALES

bowhead whale

Whales are some of the most amazing mammals in the world.

Bowhead whales have the longest life-span of any animal and often live to be more than 200 years old! They also have the largest mouth of any animal on the planet.

Size: 59 feet (18 m) long
Home: Arctic waters
Diet: crustaceans

Humpback whales make the longest migration of any mammal in the world. These whales spend most of their time in cold Arctic water, but during the winter, they swim 5,000 miles (8,050 km) to warmer water. However, individual humpback whales have been known to make journeys nearly twice this length!

Size: 52.5 feet (16 m) long
Home: warm, shallow ocean waters
Diet: krill and small fish

humpback whale

MAMMALS IN DANGER

Many of the mammals you've seen in this book are in danger of becoming <u>extinct</u>.

One problem facing these animals is <u>global warming</u>, which could cause the habitats of many mammals to disappear and make it difficult for them to survive. Global warming causes the ice that polar bears live on to melt and areas in Africa where zebras graze to become dry and desert-like. This makes it difficult for these mammals to find food.

Electricity and other types of energy are made by burning fossil fuels, which are substances that take millions of years to form naturally. When we burn these fossil fuels, certain gases are released into the atmosphere that make it difficult for heat to leave the planet. This is what is causing global warming—but you can help stop it!

By using less electricity and recycling as much as possible, you can help save many animals from becoming extinct.

Try these energy-saving tips:

• Turn off all lights and electrical devices when you aren't using them.

• Ride your bike or walk as much as possible.

• Take all of your paper and plastic waste to a recycling center.

FIND OUT MORE

BOOKS

Mammals
by Rose Inserra
(Gareth Stevens Publishing, 2010)

Mammals
by Grace Jones
(BookLife, 2016)

WEBSITES

BBC NATURE
www.bbc.co.uk/nature/life/mammal
Discover all the different species of mammals
and their habitats.

National Geographic Kids
kids.nationalgeographic.com/animals/
hubs/mammals/

This website features photos, videos, and other interactive
content featuring many unique mammals.

GLOSSARY

adapted	changed over time to suit an environment
bloodstream	the blood moving throughout the body
blowholes	the holes on top of dolphins' or whales' heads that they use to breathe
blunt	not sharp
class	a group of animals with similar characteristics
climates	the common weather conditions in certain places
crustaceans	animals that live in water and have hard outer shells
extinct	no longer existing
fertilization	the process of causing an egg to develop into a new living thing
global warming	the slow rise of Earth's temperature, caused in part by the burning of fossil fuels
habitat	the natural home or environment in which a plant or animal lives
herd	a large group of animals that live together
limbs	the arms or legs of an animal or human
migration	the seasonal movement of animals from one area to another
nocturnal	active at night instead of during the day
organs	the parts of an animal that have specific, important jobs
oxygen	a gas that all animals need to survive
species	a group of very similar animals that are capable of producing babies together
traits	qualities or characteristics
unique	unlike anything else
vertebrate	an animal with a backbone

INDEX